PLANTS

written by David Alderton
illustrated by Studio Boni/Galante
and Ivan Stalio

Ladybird

CONTENTS

THE ORIGINS OF PLANTS

Plants first appeared on Earth about 630 million years ago, long before animals came into existence. The earliest plants developed in water, and then, around 400 million years ago, vegetation began to grow on land.

Cycads

These ancient plants, which look like a cross between ferns and trees, were already present on Earth over 200 million years ago, at the time of the dinosaurs. Cycads grow from seeds, which can be as large as a hen's egg.

Algae

The first plants were very small and simple. They were similar to **algae**, being made up of single cells. Algae are very adaptable, and can grow almost anywhere on Earth in a damp environment.

Giant sequoias

These trees are among the largest plants in the world. They can grow to over 80 metres – taller than a skyscraper. They grow mainly in northwestern America. People have cut tunnels through sequoia trunks that are wide enough to drive a car through.

WHAT ARE PLANTS?

There are over 275,000 different kinds of plants in the world today. These include mosses and liverworts, which were the first plants on land. The most important plants today are the flowering plants, which are the ones that produce seeds.

CHLOROPHYLL
This is the substance in leaves that makes them green. It also helps to make the plant's food through **photosynthesis**.

Flowers
Flowers contain sweet nectar to attract insects.

Stalk
The plant is supported by the stalk.

Leaves
These contain chlorophyll to make the plant's food.

PHOTOSYNTHESIS
Chlorophyll makes the plant's food in the leaves by combining carbon dioxide from the air, hydrogen from water and energy from the Sun.

Roots
Water and minerals from the soil are taken up by the roots.

FLOWERING PLANTS

Flowers attract creatures, such as insects, bats and birds, to **pollinate** them. Seeds form as the flower dies. The seeds then start to grow – a process called **germination** – and produce new plants.

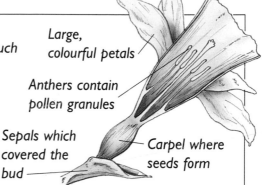

Large, colourful petals

Anthers contain pollen granules

Sepals which covered the bud

Carpel where seeds form

Parasitic plants

Mistletoe grows on the branches of trees like apple and poplar. It uses its roots to reach the tree's **xylem**, drawing off water and mineral salts from the tree rather than from the soil.

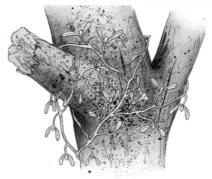

Epiphytes

Epiphytes grow on the sides of other plants. They have no roots in the soil. Instead they obtain mineral salts from rain. Bromeliads have leaves which form special cups at their centres. The cup fills up when it rains and provides the plant with water.

Mushrooms

Mushrooms and toadstools (called fungi) are not true plants. They have no chlorophyll, so they cannot produce food by photosynthesis. Instead, they feed on rotting vegetation.

THE WORLD'S FORESTS

Almost three-quarters of the Earth's land is covered with trees. They form forests which are home to many other plants and animals. Although trees exist in a wide range of **habitats**, some parts of the world, such as the far north or deserts, are too cold or dry for trees to survive.

Tropical rainforests
These are found near the Equator, where it is hot and wet. In rainforests, there can be as many as 300 different types of trees in just two square kilometres.

Deciduous forests

Deciduous trees shed their leaves in autumn, and then grow them again in spring. Deciduous forests grow where there are distinct seasons, and the weather becomes colder during the winter.

Coniferous forests

Conifers grow in cold climates. They have needles rather than leaves so that snow falls off them more easily. Conifers grow so thickly that little light can penetrate to the forest floor, and few other plants can grow there.

SURVIVAL IN THE HEAT

The burning heat of the Sun, the freezing temperatures at night and the lack of rain mean that hardly any plants can live in the world's deserts. But cacti and succulents have **evolved** to survive in these hot, dry places, and other plants spring into life in the sandy soil when it rains.

Lack of leaves
Cacti have spines rather than leaves. These reduce the amount of water lost by **transpiration**. They also give good protection against animals which might otherwise eat the cacti.

Under the ground
The roots of cacti are often shallow and extend over a wide area. This helps them to absorb the moisture which forms in the early morning as dew.

The effect of rain

There is no regular rainfall in the desert, and some places stay dry for many years. But when the rains do come, the desert landscape is transformed into a mass of colour. Seeds which have been lying in the sand since the end of the last rain germinate. They must produce plants, followed very quickly by flowers and more seeds if they are to survive until the next rain.

Long-lived plants

Succulents grow in the desert. They have thick, fleshy leaves where they store water. These desert plants grow slowly, and some can live for well over 100 years. If pieces of cacti and succulents break off, they can take root in the desert sand and grow into new plants.

SURVIVAL IN THE COLD

The ground is permanently frozen in cold northern parts of the world. During the very short summers, the top layer of soil thaws and the ground then becomes marshy. Trees cannot grow because of the frozen ground and cold summers, and the landscape looks bleak. There may be a few willow or alder bushes, and small flowering shrubs. The ground is covered with low-growing grasses, mosses, herbs and lichens.

Lichens

Lichens are the most common form of plant life in the southern continent of Antarctica, which is the coldest place on Earth. They grow very slowly wherever there is moisture and are surprisingly colourful, often being shades of pink or red.

FLOWERS

Flowering plants grow close to the ground so that the fierce winds will not damage their blooms. Annual plants which flower and die in a year are very rare in cold climates, because they cannot produce seed in time, before the snow buries them.

True partnership

Lichens are remarkable, because they are a combination of algae and fungi. The algae, which contain chlorophyll, can photosynthesise and produce food, while the fungi provide protection and minerals, so that both can survive. This kind of cooperation is called symbiosis.

Vital food

Plant-eating animals such as reindeer and Arctic hares depend on tiny plant life to survive in the cold Arctic environment.

ENJOYING THE WATER

Some plants live entirely underwater, whereas others
have leaves and flowers above the surface. The roots of
water plants are important since they act as anchors.
Water plant leaves are often long and thin or feathery.

GIANT WATER LILY
*This plant grows in the river
Amazon in South America.
Its leaves can grow to be
as wide as a bus and are
strong enough to support
the weight of a child
sitting on them.*

Pond plants
Different plants grow at different depths in water. Those round the
edge are called marginals.

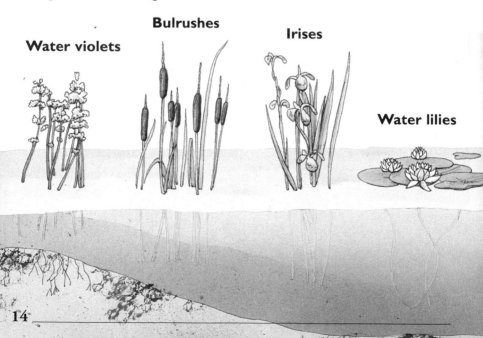

Water violets

Bulrushes

Irises

Water lilies

MANGROVE SWAMPS
These marshy areas are connected to the sea, so the mangrove trees here must grow In salty water. Some of their roots stick upwards, out of the mud, to obtain oxygen from the air at low tide.

Coastal scene

Grasses often grow in sand leading down to the seashore. They produce shoots called **rhizomes** which burrow down into the sand, stopping the plant from blowing away. Once the sand is firm, flowering plants that can live in the salty environment will start to grow. On the rocks, seaweeds (which are algae) cling fast as the tide moves in and out.

THE MEAT-EATERS

In parts of the world where the soil is boggy and has a low mineral content, strange meat-eating plants have evolved. They lure unsuspecting insects into their traps, with enticing scents and offers of sweet nectar. Even small mammals can fall into some of the larger of these plants. There they drown, and their remains are slowly digested by the plant.

Venus fly trap
Found in the swamplands of Carolina in America, this plant attracts flies to its open leaves, in the centre of which there are special trigger spikes. When the spikes are brushed by the insect, the leaves spring shut in a fraction of a second, trapping the fly.

Sarracenia
This plant is like a hollow tube. Flies and other insects crawl onto the rim of the plant. They lose their grip and tumble down inside, unable to escape.

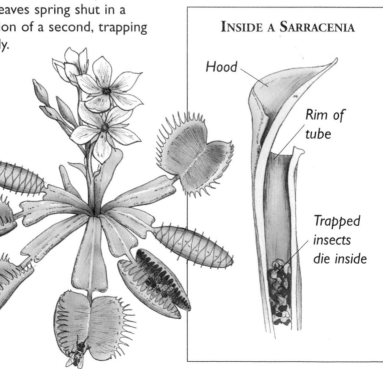

INSIDE A SARRACENIA

Hood

Rim of tube

Trapped insects die inside

Sundews

This group of plants grows throughout the world. Their sticky appearance lures insects down onto their leaves. But once a fly lands here, it will be unable to escape. It dies, and its body is slowly digested by the plant.

Pitcher plants

These plants come in many different shapes and sizes to attract insects into their pitchers, and they may fill up with rainwater. Some pitcher plants may grow to a height of 10 metres by climbing up trees, whereas others stay much closer to the ground.

A SILVER FIR TREE

A silver fir tree, like most conifer trees, does not change through the year. Its leaves do not lose their green coloration and they do not fall off. Conifers are most common in colder parts of the world. Conifers grow taller than any other trees. A redwood in the Redwood National Park in California, America, is the tallest tree on Earth. It measures over 111 metres in height – more than eighteen giraffes! Conifers also live longer than most other trees. Bristlecone pine trees could have a maximum lifespan of about 5,500 years.

PLANTATIONS

Conifers are grown commercially in plantations both as a source of timber and for the paper industry. They are also grown as Christmas trees, a fashion started by Queen Victoria's husband, Prince Albert, in the 19th century.

GROWING AND SPREADING

Many flowering plants use seeds to reproduce. Some plants can also divide from their roots or stems, buds or leaves, to reproduce. This is called **vegetative reproduction**. It allows plants to spread more rapidly than is possible from seed.

Bulbs

An onion is a bulb. If you slice it in half, you will see it is made up of tightly-packed leaves. A bulb is actually a type of bud. Roots grow out from the base of the bulb, with new bulbs developing on the sides.

Tubers

Some plants, like potatoes, have underground stems which swell at their ends to form **tubers**. If you look closely at a potato, you will be able to see the scar where it was attached to a stem when it was underground.

Creepers

Epiphytic orchids grow by creeping along tree branches, using their roots to anchor themselves to the tree.

THE FLOWERING CYCLE

For a seed to form, pollen from the male part of the plant must reach the female part. This can be done within the same plant, and is called self-pollination. More often, two plants are involved, which is known as cross-pollination. Insects often help to pollinate plants, and other creatures also play a part, such as nectar-feeding birds that transfer pollen between flowers. When you look inside a flower, you can usually see the pollen. This is present on the **stamen**, and looks like powder.

Wind pollination

Some plants such as grasses and many trees depend on the wind rather than insects for pollination. Their flowers are very small and they have no nectar. The pollen granules are very light, and are produced in huge quantities. You can become allergic to this type of pollen, and suffer from hay fever as a result.

Insect pollination

Many flowers have coloured petals to attract insects. When an insect comes to feed on the flower's nectar, its head brushes against the male anther, collecting pollen. When the insect lands on another flower of the same species, it rubs this pollen onto the female **stigma** and pollination occurs.

Sycamore seeds

Sycamore leaves

Oak leaves

Pine needles

Seed dispersal

Sycamore seeds are kept in capsules that fly long distances in the wind. Pine cones fall to the ground and the seeds spill onto the soil. Squirrels carry acorns away from the oak tree to places where they may grow.

Acorns

Pine cones

Coconuts

Some seeds can be carried long distances. A coconut is the seed of a palm tree, which often grows near the sea. The coconut may fall into the sea and be washed up on an island, where it grows.

Helpful birds

Birds often eat fruits, and although they digest the soft part, the seeds are left intact. The bird will then pass the seeds out in its droppings, often a long way from where it ate the fruit. This helps plants to spread.

PROTECTION AND WEAPONS

Plants cannot move like animals can – they are held in the ground by their roots. So they must develop other ways to protect themselves and avoid being eaten by grazing animals. Many plants have sharp spines to stop animals eating them.

Bramble

The spikes on bramble shoots form a thick barrier, which allows the plant to grow over a wide area.

Sharp spikes break off like splinters.

Even the leaves have small spikes on their undersides.

Acacias

Acacias grow quickly, protected by
a dense covering of vicious spines.
Once the acacia is mature, with
no lower branches, only the
tall giraffe can reach its
leaves. The giraffe's mouth
is not injured by the spikes.

Deadly nightshade

Some plants protect themselves
by being poisonous. The
poisonous berries of deadly
nightshade may look tempting,
but they can kill you if swallowed.

Nettles

The caterpillars of some
butterflies feed on stinging
nettles. This might give
them some protection
against predators.

Why Nettles Sting

This close-up picture shows the
sharp spiky hairs on a nettle leaf.
If you touch the leaf, the hairs break
off and release painful formic acid into your
skin. Cutting nettles back regularly strengthens
their stinging power.

PLANTS UNDER THREAT

Whole communities of plants are being destroyed every day all over the world, particularly in tropical parts. Huge areas of forest are being cleared to supply timber, often for furniture, and little is being done to replant these forests. The trees take many years to grow, so some of them are becoming endangered. Trees are also often cut to provide firewood.

Growing firewood

Some trees are now being planted specially for the purpose of providing fuel, to conserve forests. The neem tree was taken to Ghana in Africa from India in the early 1900s. Today it is widely grown, and bats feeding on its fruits have spread its seeds and helped to establish it over a large area.

TRADE IN PLANTS

Although plants can be cultivated in nurseries, some, like cacti, are slow to grow and can take many years to reach a large size. People therefore search for large specimens in the wild and dig them up. There are laws which prohibit the sale of endangered wild plants, but it is difficult to enforce these laws.

Firewood

In many areas trees are vital as the only available fuel. Wood is still frequently used for cooking and heating, particularly in developing countries.

PLANT BREEDING

People have been breeding plants and selecting the best ones for many years. This has led to a wide range of cultivated crops and plants which we have in our gardens and homes. **Strains** have been developed which are more resistant to disease, and will grow well in colder parts of the world. Crosses between two strains produce what are called first generation **hybrids**. These often grow better and produce bigger crops.

Decorative plants
New strains of plants are tested by commercial nurseries to ensure they will grow well before they are made available to the public. Trials of this type can last for several years. Plant scientists are now starting to alter the colours of flowers as well as the size, to give a greater variety of plants to be grown in the house or garden.

New crops

Cereal crops are very important sources of food, and farmers prefer strains which have high yields. But it is still important to keep older less productive seeds available, in case the crops of today are hit by diseases and new strains have to be developed.

Seed banks

These have been established to store rarer varieties of cereals and plants which could be needed in the future. The International Maize and Wheat Improvement Centre in Mexico keeps 120,000 different strains of these two cereals.

PLANTS WE USE

We depend on plants in many areas of our lives. People still use reeds and timber to build their homes in some parts of the world, and baskets, bags and other household objects can be woven from plant materials, as can floor coverings. Plants are used in many of our drinks, ranging from ginger beer to tea leaves and coffee beans. Hops are grown specially to make beer. There is still much to be learnt about plants, in terms of their medicinal uses. Western scientists are now working with rainforest people to learn about the plants they use for healing purposes. This is called **ethnobotany**.

Crops

For thousands of years, people all over the world have grown crops to provide a variety of foods. These range from wheat for making bread to sunflowers for sunflower oil. The crops are grown in huge fields and are harvested at the end of the summer.

Medicines

Many of the drugs used to treat illnesses today originated from plants. Digitalis, which is found in foxgloves, is actually very poisonous but is used to treat some heart patients. The use of plants for healing purposes is called **herbalism**.

Perfumes

Roses and some other plants contain special oils which can be distilled and concentrated into perfumes. A number of these 'essential essences' are also used in lotions and ointments to help people with stress.

Insecticides

Plants have developed ways of avoiding attacks by insects. Pyrethrin is a chemical present in a type of flower called a chrysanthemum. It is deadly to insects, but does not cause serious harm to most other creatures. It is now used as an **insecticide**.

Clothing and dyes

For centuries, plant fibres such as cotton and flax have been made into clothes. Some plants, such as woad, produce dyes which are used to colour cloth and, in some cultures, for body painting.

AMAZING PLANT FACTS

- **Deadly competition** Guayle plants, which grow in groups in the desert areas of Mexico, Central America produce an acid from their roots which kills off other vegetation, preventing other plants growing near them.

- **Drought resistant** Both the caper plant, which grows in the Sahara desert in Africa, and the American pygmy cedar can live without taking up any water at all through their roots. They are able to absorb water vapour directly from the air.

- **Under threat** More than 25,000 of the world's flowering plants are now in danger of extinction, which is about one in ten of the total number of plants on the planet.

- **Tree house** The baobab tree has a huge swollen trunk, which is quite soft. In parts of Africa and Australia, people sometimes hollow this out, so that they can make a home inside the tree.

- **Largest leaves** The raffia palm, which grows on islands in the Indian Ocean, has leaves up to twenty metres long.

- **Biggest seed** The Coco de Mer palm, which grows only on the Seychelles islands off the coast of Africa, produces huge nuts which can weigh twenty kilograms. There are both male and female forms of this palm. Only the females produce these huge nuts, with pollen being produced by the male palms.

- **What a stinker!** The flowers of the rafflesia plant, which grows in the rainforests of southeast Asia, smell like rotting flesh. The flowers are huge – the biggest flowers in the world.

- **Old timer** A bristlecone pine tree in the White Mountains of California, America, is thought to be around 4,700 years old.

GLOSSARY

Algae Microscopic plants which often grow in water.

Dendrochronology The technique of finding a tree's age by counting the rings in its trunk.

Epiphyte A plant that grows on the branches of another plant and doesn't take root in the soil.

Ethnobotany The study by scientists to discover new medicines from plants.

Evolve To change gradually over many years.

Germinate The process which results in seeds sprouting and growing.

Habitat The area where a plant naturally grows.

Herbalism The use of plants for healing purposes.

Hybrid A plant which is produced by crossing two similar but different plants.

Insecticide A chemical used to kill harmful insects and pests which often damage crops.

Photosynthesis The process which allows plants to make their food from sunlight.

Pollinate The transfer of pollen to the stigma which fertilizes the flower.

Rhizome An underground stem present in some plants which helps them to spread.

Seedling A young plant, grown from a seed.

Stamen The male part of a flower where pollen is produced.

Stigma The female part of the flower where pollination takes place.

Strain A plant which has been grown under special conditions for a particular purpose.

Transpiration Evaporation of water from tiny holes, called pores, in the leaves.

Tuber A short, fleshy underground stem.

Vegetative reproduction The way in which some plants can increase in numbers by growing from existing parts of the plant.

Xylem The system that carries water and mineral salts from the roots to other parts of the plant.

INDEX *(Entries in* **bold** *refer to an illustration)*